DESERT LIGHT

DESERT LIGHT

MYTHS AND VISIONS
OF THE GREAT SOUTHWEST

PHOTOGRAPHS BY DEAN LEE UHLINGER

EDITED BY JOHN MILLER

CHRONICLE BOOKS
SAN FRANCISCO

Library of Congress Cataloging-in-Publication Data

Uhlinger, Dean Lee.

     Desert light : myths and visions of the great Southwest /
photographs by Dean Lee Uhlinger ; edited by John Miller.

     p. cm.

     ISBN 0-8118-0211-6 (pbk.)

     1. Indians of North America—Southwest, New—Religion and mythology.
2. Southwest, New—Pictorial works. I. Miller, John, 1959- . II. Title.

     E78.S7U38 1992

     299'.7979—dc20   92-12828

                                     CIP

Printed in Singapore.

Distributed by Raincoast books, 112 East Third Ave.,
Vancouver, B.C. V5T 1C8

10 9 8 7 6 5 4 3 2 1

CHRONICLE BOOKS

275 FIFTH STREET

SAN FRANCISCO, CA 94103

TABLE OF CONTENTS

INTRODUCTION

Peter Nabokov

A creation story is a printout of a culture's sacred constitution, an X-ray of their persistent identity, a window into their collective soul. In these excerpts from lengthy origin myths derived from desert-dwelling Indian peoples, the fact that we outsiders were never originally meant to read them, much less overhear them, suggests their intended, hidden agendas. Aimed at other ears, set within contexts of other cultures passing on ultimate wisdom among themselves, their goals were more urgent than mere entertainment—which never prevented listeners from howling with laughter whenever a Trickster Creator made a botch of forming their specific world.

Origin stories like these were recited to renew the universe during major rituals in the seasonal year; they were told to remind tribespeople how their immediate

topography had acquired its particular twists and turns;

they were narrated in the midst of key initiation

ceremonies which transformed free-playing children into

serious adults who thereby became responsible to social

communities and tribal cosmologies; they were chanted to

conjure up all manner of prototypical events after which

humans might model their own actions; they were related

to draw cosmic time and forces into the performative

present so as to convince people that theirs was sacred

history. Such narratives, we must never forget, were

everywhere regarded as first and last word—absolute truth.

And yet they are also almost divine soap operas at

times, complex archetypal family plots that broke rules

and evoked original jealousies, dissents, angers, breaches of conduct, and heartless paybacks. In the mesa-and-pinion landscape of these selections, certain great beings reappear again and again: nurturing Spider, the sacred twins or "Twain," ancient insects, and, of course, that ambivalent fellow, Coyote, ramshackling his way through primordia. There are also recurrent themes: emergence from under-worlds and the always pervasive romance with moisture.

Sometimes these desert myths open with a swirling of pre-dawn vapors, perhaps there is a shallow sink where moisture jells into emerald-colored sludge—the primal bubbling of what will someday be you and me. A delight arises from the pre-human, the pre-everything. What is it about these Great American hardscrabble lands (where one imagines the anonymous but once so living-breathing-thinking-working-laughing-loving retellers of these creation stories scratching for their livings) which can yield such spacey, neo-Platonic scenarios of how this earth was made and all beings upon it? First off, where Indians are concerned (and probably a lot else) we must always question our questions. For these Pimas and Sias and Navajos lived joyful lives, which they rarely remembered as raw survival or bitter hardship. Over millennia their adaptations to climate and habitat formed exciting annual rounds of hunting and foraging, sowing and harvesting, and they managed to find time for making arts, taking trips, exchanging gossip and transacting with the spirits around them. Any apparent discrepancy between the seeming spareness of their lives and the imaginative range and depth of their creation narratives is our problem, never theirs.

And who knows what old knowledge lies safely encoded in these wondrous accounts? To have one Pima creation story, for instance, feature that humble, denigrated weed we call the creosote bush and then to read recent research that their gradually widening circles of roots are older than the 5,000 year-old Bristlecone Pines from which all tree-ring dating derives, is such sweet irony. More to the point, the Pima could have cared less about our privileging of such a chronology—theirs was truly a numinous landscape. In all these stories the desert has no hourly clock, no monthly calendar: Its seasons fairly spring to life as first born and ever present.

THE CREATION OF THE WORLD

Pima

In the beginning there was nothing at all except

darkness. All was darkness and emptiness. For a

long, long while, the darkness gathered until it

became a great mass. Over this the spirit of Earth

Doctor drifted to and fro like a fluffy bit of cotton

in the breeze. Then Earth Doctor decided to make

for himself an abiding place. So he thought within

himself, "Come forth, some kind of plant," and

there appeared the creosote bush. He placed this

before him and set it upright. But it at once fell

over. He set it upright again; again it fell. So it

fell until the fourth time it remained upright. Then

Earth Doctor took from his breast a little dust and

flattened it into a cake. When the dust cake was

still, he danced upon it, singing a magic song.

Next he created some black insects which

made black gum on the creosote bush. Then he

made a termite which worked with the small earth

cake until it grew very large. As he sang and danced

upon it, the flat world stretched out on all sides

until it was as large as it is now. Then he made a

round sky-cover to fit over it, round like the houses

of the Pimas. But the earth shook and stretched,

so that it was unsafe. So Earth Doctor made a gray

spider which was to spin a web around the edges of

the earth and sky, fastening them together. When

this was done, the earth grew firm and solid.

Earth Doctor made water, mountains, trees,

grass, and weeds—made everything as we see it now.

But all was still inky blackness. Then he made a

dish, poured water into it, and it became ice. He

threw this round block of ice far to the north, and

it fell at the place where the earth and sky were

woven together. At once the ice began to gleam and

shine. We call it now the sun. It rose from the

ground in the north up into the sky and then fell

back. Earth Doctor took it and threw it to the west

where the earth and sky were sewn together. It rose

into the sky and again slid back to the earth. Then

he threw it to the far south, but it slid back again

to the flat earth. Then at last he threw it to the

east. It rose higher and higher in the sky until it

reached the highest point in the round blue cover

and began to slide down on the other side. And so

the sun does even yet.

Then Earth Doctor poured more water into

the dish and it became ice. He sang a magic song,

and threw the round ball of ice to the north where

the earth and sky are woven together. It gleamed

and shone, but not so brightly as the sun. It became

the moon, and it rose in the sky, but fell back

again, just as the sun had done. So he threw the

ball to the west, and then to the south, but it slid

back each time to the earth. Then he threw it to

the east, and it rose to the highest point in the

sky-cover and began to slide down on the other side.

And so it does even today, following the sun.

But Earth Doctor saw that when the sun and

moon were not in the sky, all was inky darkness.

So he sang a magic song, and took some water into

his mouth and blew it into the sky, in a spray, to

make little stars. Then he took his magic crystal

and broke it into pieces and threw them into the

sky, to make the larger stars. Next he took his

walking stick and placed ashes on the end of it.

Then he drew it across the sky to form the Milky

Way. So Earth Doctor made all the stars.

ORIGIN OF THE SAGUARO
AND PALO VERDE CACTI

Pima

Once upon a time an old Indian woman had two

grandchildren. Every day she ground wheat and

corn between the grinding stones to make porridge

for them. One day as she put the water-olla on the

fire outside the house to heat the water, she told the

children not to quarrel because they might upset the

olla. But the children began to quarrel. They upset

the olla and spilled the water and their grandmother

spanked them.

    Then the children were angry and ran away.

They ran far away over the mountains. The grand-

mother heard them whistling and she ran after them

and followed them from place to place, but she

could not catch up with them.

At last the older boy said, "I will turn into

a saguaro, so that I shall live forever and bear fruit

every summer."

The younger said, "Then I will turn into a

palo verde and stand there forever. These mountains

are so bare and have nothing on them but rocks.

I will make them green."

The old woman heard the cactus whistling

and recognized the voice of her grandson. So she

went up to it and tried to take the prickly thing

into her arms, but the thorns killed her.

That is how the saguaro and the palo verde

came to be on the mountains and the desert.

ORIGIN OF THE RAVEN AND THE MACAW

(TOTEMS OF SUMMER AND WINTER)

Z u n i

The priest who was named Yanauluha carried ever

in his hand a staff which now in the daylight was

plumed and covered with feathers—yellow, blue-green,

red, white, black, and varied. Attached to it were

shells, which made a song-like tinkle. The people

when they saw it stretched out their hands and

asked many questions.

   Then the priest balanced it in his hand, and

struck with it a hard place, and blew upon it.

Amid the plumes appeared four round things—

mere eggs they were. Two were blue like the sky

and two dun-red like the flesh of the Earth-mother.

Then the people asked many questions.

"These," said the priests, "are the seed of

living beings. Choose which ye will follow.

From two eggs shall come beings of beautiful

plumage, colored like the grass and fruits of

summer. Where they fly and ye follow, shall al-

ways be summer. Without toil, fields of food shall

flourish. And from the other two eggs shall come

evil beings, piebald with white, without colors.

And where these two shall fly and ye shall

follow, winter strives with summer. Only by labor

shall the fields yield fruit, and your children and theirs

shall strive for the fruits. Which do ye choose?"

"The blue! The blue!" cried the people, and

those who were strongest carried off the blue eggs,

leaving the red eggs to those who waited. They laid

the blue eggs with much gentleness in soft sand on

the sunny side of a hill, watching day by day.

They were precious of color; surely they would be

the precious birds of the Summer-land. Then the

eggs cracked and the birds came out, with open eyes

and pinfeather under their skins.

"We chose wisely," said the people. "Yellow

and blue, red and green, are their dresses, even seen

through their skins." So they fed them freely of all

the foods which men favor. Thus they taught them

to eat all desirable food. But when the feathers

appeared, they were black with white bandings.

They were ravens. And they flew away croaking

hoarse laughs and mocking our fathers.

But the other eggs became beautiful macaws,

and were wafted by a toss of the priest's wand to

the faraway Summer-land.

So those who had chosen the raven, became the Raven People. They were the Winter People and they were many and strong. But those who had chosen the macaw, became the Macaw People. They were the Summer People, and few in number, and less strong, but they were wiser because they were more deliberate. The priest Yanauluha, being wise, became their father, even as the Sun-father is among the little moons of the sky. He and his sisters were the ancestors of the priest-keepers of things.

THE COURSE OF THE SUN

S i a

Sussistinnako, the spider, said to the sun,

    "My son, you will ascend and pass over the

world above. You will go from north to south.

Return and tell me what you think of it."

    The sun said, on his return, "Mother, I did

as you bade me, and I did not like the road."

    Spider told him to ascend and pass over the

world from west to the east. On his return, the sun said,

    "It may be good for some, mother, but I did

not like it."

Spider said, "You will again ascend and pass

over the straight road from east to the west. Return

and tell me what you think of it."

That night the sun said, "I am much contented.

I like that road much."

Sussistinnako said, "My son, you will ascend

each day and pass over the world from east to west."

Upon each day's journey the sun stops midway

from the east to the center of the world to eat his

breakfast. In the center he stops to eat his dinner.

Halfway from the center to the west he stops to eat

his supper. He never fails to eat these three meals

each day, and always stops at the same points.

The sun wears a shirt of dressed deerskin,

with leggings of the same reaching to his thighs.

The shirt and leggings are fringed. His moccasins

are also of deerskin and embroidered in yellow, red,

and turquoise beads. He wears a kilt of deerskin,

having a snake painted upon it. He carries a bow

and arrows, the quiver being of cougar skin, hanging

over his shoulder, and he holds his bow in his left

hand and an arrow in his right. He always wears the

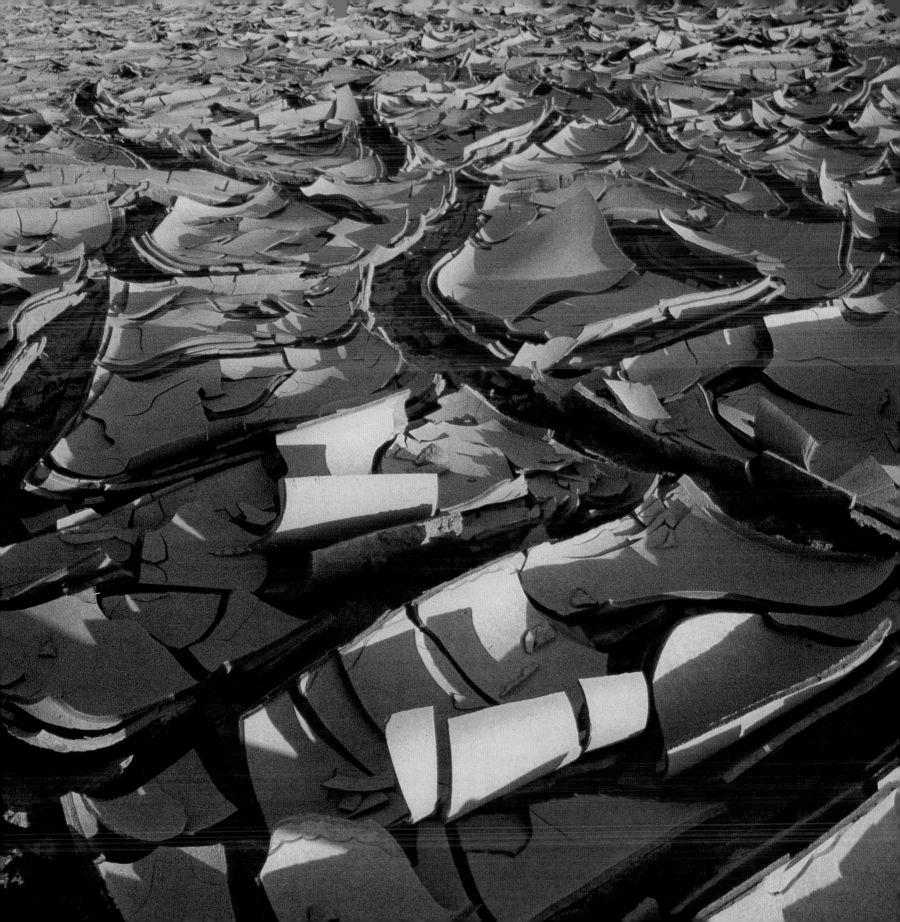

mask which protects him from the sight of the

people of Ha-arts.

At the top of the mask is an eagle plume

with parrot plumes; an eagle plume is at each

side, and one at the bottom of the mask. The

hair around the head and face is red like fire,

and when it moves and shakes people cannot

look closely at the mask. It is not intended that

they should observe closely, else they would

know that instead of seeing the sun they see

only his mask.

The moon came to the upper world with the

sun and he also wears a mask.

Each night the sun passes by the house of

Sussistinnako, the spider, who asks him, "How are

my children above? How many have died today?

How many have been born today?" The sun lingers

only long enough to answer his questions. He then

passes on to his house in the east.

HASJELTI AND HOSTJOGHON

Navajo

Hasjelti was the son of the white corn, and

Hostjoghon the son of the yellow corn. They were

born on the mountains where the fogs meet. These

two became the great song-makers of the world.

To the mountain where they were born

[Henry Mountain, Utah], they gave two songs and

two prayers. Then they went to Sierra Blanca

[Colorado] and made two songs and prayers and

dressed the mountain in clothing of white shell with

two eagle plumes upon its head. They visited San

Mateo Mountain [New Mexico] and gave to it two

songs and prayers, and dressed it in turquoise, even

to leggings and moccasins, and placed two eagle

plumes upon its head. Then they went to San

Francisco Mountain [Arizona] and made two songs

and prayers and dressed that mountain in abalone

shells with two eagle plumes upon its head. They

then visited Ute Mountain and gave to it two songs

and prayers and dressed it in black beads. Then they

returned to their own mountain where the fogs meet

and said, "We two have made all these songs."

Other brothers were born of the white corn

and yellow corn, and two brothers were placed on

each mountain. They are the spirits of the moun-

tains and to them the clouds come first. All the

brothers together made game, the deer and elk and

buffalo, and so game was created.

Navajos pray for rain and snow to Hasjelti

and Hostjoghon. They stand upon the mountain

tops and call the clouds to gather around them.

Hasjelti prays to the sun, for the Navajos.

"Father, give me the light of your mind that

my mind may be strong. Give me your strength, that

my arm may be strong. Give me your rays, that corn

and other vegetation may grow."

The most important prayers are addressed to

Hasjelti and the most valuable gifts made to him.

He talks to the Navajos through the birds, and for

this reason the choicest feathers and plumes are

placed in the cigarettes and attached to the prayer

sticks offered to him.

THE CLOUD PEOPLE

S i a

Now all the Cloud People, the Lightning People,

the Thunder and Rainbow Peoples followed the

Sia into the upper world. But all the people of

Tinia, the middle world, did not leave the lower

world. Only a portion were sent by the Spider to

work for the people of the upper world. The Cloud

People are so many that, although the demands of

the earth people are so great, there are always many

passing about over Tinia for pleasure. These Cloud

People ride on wheels, small wheels being used by

the little Cloud children and large wheels by the

older ones.

The Cloud People keep always behind their

masks. The shape of the mask depends upon the

number of the people and the work being done.

The Henati are the floating white clouds behind

which the Cloud People pass for pleasure. The

Heash are clouds like the plains and behind these

the Cloud People are laboring to water the earth.

Water is brought by the Cloud People, from the

springs at the base of the mountains, in gourds

and jugs and vases by the men, women, and children.

They rise from the springs and pass through the

trunk of the tree to its top, which reaches Tinia.

They pass on to the point to be sprinkled.

The priest of the Cloud People is above even

the priests of the Thunder, Lightning, and Rainbow

Peoples. The Cloud People have ceremonials, just

like those of the Sia. On the altars of the Sia may

be seen figures arranged just as the Cloud People sit

in their ceremonials.

When a priest of the Cloud People wishes

assistance from the Thunder and Lightning Peoples,

he notifies their priests, but keeps a supervision of

all things himself.

Then the Lightning People shoot their arrows

to make it rain the harder. The smaller flashes come

from the bows of the children. The Thunder People

have human forms, with wings of knives, and by

flapping these wings they make a great noise. Thus

they frighten the Cloud and Lightning People into

working the harder.

The Rainbow People were created to work in

Tinia to make it more beautiful for the people of

Ha-arts, the earth, to look upon. The elders make

the beautiful rainbows, but the children assist.

The Sia have no idea of what or how these bows

are made. They do know, however, that war heroes

always travel upon the rainbows.

RAIN SONG

S i a

White floating clouds. Clouds, like the plains, come

and water the earth. Sun, embrace the earth that she

may be fruitful. Moon, lion of the north, bear of

the west, badger of the south, wolf of the east, eagle

of the heavens, shrew of the earth, elder war hero,

younger war hero, warriors of the six mountains of

the world, intercede with the Cloud People for us

that they may water the earth. Medicine bowl,

cloud bowl, and water vase, give us your hearts, that

the earth may be watered. I make the ancient road

of meal that my song may pass straight over it—the

ancient road. White shell bead woman who lives

where the sun goes down, mother whirlwind, father

Sussistinnako, mother Yaya, creator of good

thoughts, yellow woman of the north, blue woman

of the west, red woman of the south, white woman

of the east, slightly yellow woman of the zenith, and

dark woman of the nadir, I ask your intercession

with the Cloud People.

RAIN SONG

S i a

We, the ancient ones, ascended from the middle of

the world below, through the door of the entrance

to the lower world. We hold our songs to the

Cloud, Lightning, and Thunder Peoples as we hold

our own hearts. Our medicine is precious.

[Addressing the people of Tinia:]

We entreat you to send your thoughts to us

so that we may sing your songs straight, so that they

will pass over the straight road to the Cloud priests

that they may cover the earth with water, so that she

may bear all that is good for us.

Lightning People, send your arrows to the

middle of the earth. Hear the echo! Who is it?

The People of the Spruce of the North. All your

people and your thoughts come to us. Who is it?

People of the white floating Clouds. Your thoughts

come to us. All your people and your thoughts

come to us. Who is it? The Lightning People.

Your thoughts come to us. Who is it? Cloud

People at the horizon. All your people and your

thoughts come to us.

RAIN SONG

S i a

Let the white floating clouds—the clouds like the

plains—the Lightning, Thunder, Rainbow, and

Cloud Peoples, water the earth. Let the People of

the White Floating Clouds—the People of the

Clouds like the Plains—the Lightning, Thunder,

Rainbow, and Cloud Peoples—come and work for

us, and water the earth.

COYOTE PLACES THE STARS

Wasco

One time there were five wolves, all brothers, who

traveled together. Whatever meat they got when

they were hunting they would share with Coyote. One

evening Coyote saw the wolves looking up at the sky.

"What are you looking at up there, my

brothers?" asked Coyote.

"Oh, nothing," said the oldest wolf.

Next evening Coyote saw they were all

looking up in the sky at something. He asked the

next oldest wolf what they were looking at, but he

wouldn't say. It went on like this for three or four

nights. No one wanted to tell Coyote what they

were looking at because they thought he would want

to interfere. One night Coyote asked the youngest

wolf brother to tell him, and the youngest wolf said

to the other wolves, "Let's tell Coyote what we see

up there. He won't do anything."

So they told him. "We see two animals up

there. Way up there, where we cannot get to them."

"Let's go up and see them," said Coyote.

"Well, how can we do that?"

"Oh, I can do that easy," said Coyote. "I

can show you how to get up there without any

trouble at all."

Coyote gathered a great number of arrows

and then began shooting them into the sky. The

first arrow stuck in the sky and the second arrow

stuck in the first. Each arrow stuck in the end of

the one before it like that until there was a ladder

reaching down to the earth.

"We can climb up now," said Coyote.

The oldest wolf took his dog with him, and then

the other four wolf brothers came, and then Coyote.

They climbed all day and into the night. All the

next day they climbed. For many days and nights

they climbed, until finally they reached the sky.

They stood in the sky and looked over at the two

animals the wolves had seen from down below.

They were two grizzly bears.

"Don't go near them," said Coyote.

"They will tear you apart." But the two youngest

wolves were already headed over. And the next two

youngest wolves followed them. Only the oldest

wolf held back. When the wolves got near the grizzlies, nothing happened. The wolves sat down and looked at the bears, and the bears sat there looking at the wolves. The oldest wolf, when he saw it was safe, came over with his dog and sat down with them.

Coyote wouldn't come over. He didn't trust the bears. "That makes a nice picture, though," thought Coyote. "They all look pretty good sitting there like that. I think I'll leave it that way for everyone to see. Then when people look at them in the sky they will say, 'There's a story about that picture,' and they will tell a story about me."

So Coyote left it that way. He took out the

arrows as he descended so there was no way for

anyone to get back. From down on the earth Coyote

admired the arrangement he had left up there.

Today they still look the same. They call those stars

Big Dipper now. If you look up there you'll see that

three wolves make up the handle and the oldest wolf,

the one in the middle, still has his dog with him. The

two youngest wolves make up the part of the bowl

under the handle, and the two grizzlies make up the

other side, the one that points toward the North Star.

When Coyote saw how they looked, he

wanted to put up a lot of stars. He arranged stars

all over the sky in pictures and then made the Big

Road across the sky with the stars he had left over.

When Coyote was finished he called

Meadowlark over. "My brother," he said, "When I

am gone, tell everyone that when they look up into

the sky and see the stars arranged this way, I was

the one who did that. That is my work."

Now Meadowlark tells that story about Coyote.

LOCATIONS